Being a BONUS mom is...

A gift for the BONUS mom to encourage and
thank you for the place that you hold.

Being a BONUS mom is an

opportunity of a lifetime.

Being a BONUS mom is possibly one of the hardest jobs on the planet.

Being a BONUS mom is

knowing never-ending

feelings of inadequacy.

Being a BONUS mom is

always feeling compared.

Being a BONUS mom is learning to be the bigger person.

Being a BONUS mom is

the amazing privilege of

loving someone who needs

extra love and stability.

Being a BONUS mom is

intimidating.

Being a BONUS mom is

important.

Being a BONUS mom is many times a balancing act more difficult than walking the high-wire.

Being a BONUS mom is a

great deal of trust

bestowed on you by

another person.

Being a BONUS mom is
happy tears when they
present a Mother's Day
gift, and this time it is for
you.

Being a BONUS mom is

opening your heart freely

and wholly.

Being a BONUS mom is encouraging love and healthy respect for all parents.

Being a BONUS mom is being in a position to be a positive example.

Being a BONUS mom is

wishing you had been

there for all the

milestones.

Being a BONUS mom is
being sad when hearing so
many baby memories.

Being a BONUS mom is thankfulness for years of not being responsible for dirty diapers.

Being a BONUS mom is

being excited for building

future moments together.

Being a BONUS mom is an exercise in tuning out the criticisms of others.

Being a BONUS mom is

messy.

Being a BONUS mom is waking up one day and realizing family relationships finally feel natural.

Being a BONUS mom is

working toward a rhythm

of togetherness.

Being a BONUS mom is

accepting responsibilities

as a parent.

Being a BONUS mom is a
great honor to be loved in
return.

Being a BONUS mom is

beautiful.

Being a BONUS mom is

offering to help make

Mother's Day gifts for

someone else. Every year.

Being a BONUS mom is
experiencing excitement
at being asked to help on
those first school
projects.

Being a BONUS mom is like a box of crayons: full of colorful choices that can create a beautiful family picture.

Being a BONUS mom is

like being on the ocean:

sometimes calm,

sometimes rough, but a

worthwhile adventure.

Being a BONUS mom is a

learning experience.

Being a BONUS mom is a

journey of grace, for

yourself and others.

Being a BONUS mom is

something that takes a

very special person, like

you.

Being a BONUS mom is

learning all of their

favorite things.

Being a BONUS mom is to

forgive yourself and

others for mistakes.

Being a BONUS mom is

NOT a competition.

Being a BONUS mom is

making room for everyone.

Being a BONUS mom is

choosing to love

unconditionally.

Being a BONUS mom is
like nothing else you will
ever do.

Being a BONUS mom is

being intentional.

Being a BONUS mom is

thinking of extra-special

or creative gifts.

Being a BONUS mom is

being available.

Being a BONUS mom is

like putting together a

life-sized puzzle.

Being a BONUS mom is

your superpower.